HERO OF BATTLE ROCK

Books by Bert Webber

The Pacific Northwest in Books (1967)
>   A bibliography of currently available books for teachers and librarians on the history and development of the Pacific Northwest and Northwest Coast
>   (Out of print)

Beachcombing for Driftwood, for Glass Floats, For Agates, for Fun. (1973)
>   Oregon Coast recreation
>   (Four printings)
>   (Out of print)

What Happened at Bayocean — Is Salishan Next? (1973)
>   Documentary on Oregon coastal erosion
>   (Expanded edition, 1974)

The Hero of Battle Rock (1973)
>   Indians attack small group of men during first attempt to settle at Port Orford on Oregon coast in 1851
>   (Expanded edition, 1978)

Oregon's Great Train Holdup - the DeAutremont Case (1973)
>   The last great train holdup of the West
>   (Expanded edition, 1974)

RETALIATION: Japanese Attacks and Allied Countermeasures on the Pacific Coast in World War II (1975)
>   Oregon State Univ. Studies in History No. 6
>   (Second printing, 1976)

Swivel-Chair Logger: The Life and Work of Anton A. Lausmann (1976)
>   A different kind of book about Oregon's timber industry
>   (Second printing, 1977)

By Bert and Margie Webber

Beachcombing and Camping Along the Northwest Coast (1978)
>   In depth approach to traditional subjects combined in one book for the first time presenting data not previously attempted

(Additional titles forthcoming)

THE HERO OF BATTLE ROCK

EXPANDED EDITION

Compiled and Edited by
BERT WEBBER

Ye Galleon Press

Fairfield, Washington

1978

Published on December 2, 1973
In Compliment to
OREGON HISTORICAL SOCIETY'S
Christmas Cheer
and
Autograph Party
by

Ye Galleon Press

ISBN 0-87770-051-6
Of This Edition Only 296 Serial
Numbered Copies Were Printed
Second Printing, February 1974
(Not Numbered)
©Bert Webber 1973, 1978
Expanded Edition January 1978

Library of Congress Cataloging in Publication Data

Kirkpatrick, J. M.
The hero of Battle Rock.

Signed, on p.   : J. M. Kirkpatrick.
Original ed., edited by O. Dodge, published in 1904 under title: The heroes of Battle Rock.
Includes index.
1. Port Orford, OR.—History. 2. Pacific coast Indians, Wars with, 1847-1865. I. Webber, Bert. II. Dodge, Orvil. III. Title.

| F884.P7K5 | 1978 | 979.5'21 | 77-26207 |

ISBN O-87770-191-1
ISBN O-87770-190-3 pbk.

(Left) "Wrong" picture? This photo appearing in major library reference books for at least seventy-five years disclaimed by descendants in 1973. "Not my grandfather !" declared Ruby Van Deventer. Photo from Gaston. (Right) John M. Kirkpatrick, born December 6, 1825, at Bush Creek, Adams County, Ohio, the "Hero of Battle Rock," shown in portrait made in Stockton, California.—from family album of Robert Kirkpatrick, a son, loaned by Evelyne Michael. (*See*: Photo Credits, p. 56.)

PREFACE TO THE 1973 PRINTING

Orvil Ovando Dodge, a Southern Oregon pioneer historian, published a twenty-one page booklet in 1904 which he entitled, *The Heroes of Battle Rock.* For content, he used Chapter III of his earlier book, *Pioneer History of Coos and Curry Counties.* This history, which had been published in 1898, was a major work and still receives acclaim now, seventy-five years later. The book, with well over five hundred pages, is listed as No. 2,495 in Smith's *Pacific Northwest Americana.*

In 1903, Dodge became manager and secretary of the Salmon Mountain Course Gold Mining Company and he brought out the booklet as a promotional piece for this mining venture. The last several pages deal with the gold mine.

A second edition of the major history, with *errata,* was published in 1969 by the Coos-Curry Pioneer and Historical Association of North Bend, Oregon. Readers with a sharp eye who have perused the history book as well as the booklet have noted that Dodge, for the 1904 booklet (Smith's No. 5,551) uses the word "Heroes" on the title page, but the singular form appears in his history as well as on the first page of the booklet. (Of course the pages about the gold mine do not

v

appear in his major work having been written five years later.) But the "hero/heroes" difference, insignificant as it may seem, is not the only cloud overhanging Dodge's work.

When Stephen D. Beckham of Coos Bay, Oregon, wrote the *errata* pages for the second edition, he had a formidable task. He acknowledged that Dodge was a "compiler" who sought data from old timers, from letters, and from the published writings of others. That there was a degree of looseness about the compilation is borne out because Beckham offers over four hundred "corrections and additions" in his *errata* pages—ten items having to do with the Battle Rock chapter.

After some careful probing, I have concluded that the material for Chapter III, "The Hero of Battle Rock," in Dodge's history, which is written in the first person and signed, "J.M. Kirkpatrick, Oro Blanco, Arizona, Nov. 29, 1897," was probably not written by the late John M. Kirkpatrick! And that John M. Kirkpatrick was probably never in Arizona! And the picture Dodge uses in his history on page 34 and again on page 184D—being one and the same—is not that of John M. Kirkpatrick!

I am indebted to Mrs. John (Evelyne Kirkpatrick) Michael—a great-granddaughter of J.M.K.—of Shingletown (Shasta County) California, who shared her geneological study with me. Then she put me in touch with Mrs. A.F. (Ruby Steele) Van Deventer—a granddaughter now in her eightys, of J.M.K.—of Crescent City, California; Dan R. Kirkpatrick—a great-grandson living in Brookings, Oregon; and Dan's son, Larry Kirkpatrick—a great-great-grandson— of Eastside (Coos County) Oregon.

Following lengthy discussions with all of these descendants, plus detailed letters between several of us for additional clarifications and reinforcement, here is what has surfaced:

John M. Kirkpatrick was a widely traveled and a very wise man in the ways of the world for his time. He was a "doer" and never a "griper." He had firm convictions. When he made up his mind on something, he stayed with it but he was open to being shown a better way. Kirkpatrick owned fast Indian ponies and the last time Ruby Van Deventer saw her grandfather "he was on that pony and going at a mighty clip with (grandfather's) hair flying in the wind!"

John Kirkpatrick did not care for hotels. He was a bed-roll camper who prided himself in his ability to live off the land. On one occasion as per habit, he raked coals of the evening campfire to one side, spread his roll upon the warm ground and retired for the night. He did not sleep long. His blanket smoldered with fire and scorched his hide causing him to scream out thus waking everybody in camp!

Evelyne Michael said, "The family is fond of saying J.M.K. hated Indians. He certainly did distrust them but note in the story that an Indian led [the Battle Rock party] up the beach to safety. I think he's join any fight for the sake of fighting. If

(Left) Rebecca Coplantz Kirkpatrick lived 69 years, John (right) 85 years. "Becky" married John when she was 22, he ten years older. They reared seven boys and three girls and spent forty-seven years as man and wife.

he was in the Southern Oregon Indian troubles it was as a civilian and not military service. His military service was for four months in 1848 during the Cayuse Indian War—three years prior to his involvement at Port Orford."

There is some belief among the descendants that he took part in the Indian/white squabbles around Table Rock, a few miles north of Medford. The Michael study includes this remark: "He could have been [at Table Rock] however I just haven't proved it either way. There is no record of J.M.K. ever killing an Indian other than during the fifteen minute Battle Rock incident."

In the course of seeking people to prepare material for his history, Dodge met Kirkpatrick and asked him to put the story of Battle Rock into writing. In the opening paragraph of Chapter III, Orvil Dodge wrote: "The compiler of this work now presents to the student of history the following interesting narrative *written by Captain J.M. Kirkpatrick...."*(Italics added.) But John, having had only a limited classroom education, according to his descendants, is believed by these descendants to have asked his brother Alfred to do the writing. Evelyne Michael wrote to me: "Alfred was John's older brother who may have written John's story and may have lived in Arizona." No other explanation for the "Oro Blanco, Arizona" in Dodge's book has come to light. Oro Blanco, Arizona and the 1897 date do not appear in the 1904 booklet. There is no record of J.M.K. ever being in Arizona, but during his travels he could have visited Alfred in Arizona, *if* Alfred lived in Arizona, which from a research standpoint has not been established.

Although John Kirkpatrick was a traveler, he was also a family man. He and his wife Rebecca Coplantz Kirkpatrick (ten years younger) had seven sons and three daughters.

Ruby Van Deventer, the only member of the family still living to have seen her grandfather wrote, "I do not believe the picture [in Dodge's book] is Grandfather Kirkpatrick." Mrs. Michael declares that the picture in the Dodge book "appears to be rather heavy set and fat, while the family thinks of John as rather lean." She said she has never seen a picture of John resembling anything like the picture labeled as Kirkpatrick in the Dodge book in any of the family picture collections. Ruby Van Deventer and Evelyne Michael provided two portraits of John M. Kirkpatrick, made at different times. He was a lean man. The "wrong" picture is believed by several of the descendants to be that of John's brother Alfred. How it came into Dodge's possession is unknown. Some think the picture is that of Captain William Tichenor but Tichenor too, was on the "lean" side.

Although much has been made of Captain Tichenor as the "founder of Port Orford" by historians, and I have no cause to detract from this, the role of John M. Kirkpatrick as the leader of Tichenor's advance party at the future townsite has all but been lost. Unfortunately, the Oregon State Parks Division did not include Kirkpatrick by name in the one-hundred-sixty-four word roadside marker for Battle Rock State Park at Port Orford.

Dodge claims the *Oregonian* published a newspaper account in 1851 in which Kirkpatrick and eight others were believed to have been murdered by Indians. The footnotes in Hubert Howe Bancroft's *History of Oregon* (Vol. XXX. p. 195) do not include the *Oregonian* but cites the *Oregon Statesman* of July 4, 1851, p. 2, column 6, and refers readers to an editorial paragraph on the same page in column 2:

MORE INDIAN MURDERS

> The communication published in another column of to-day's paper leaves little room to doubt that a party of nine persons, left at Port Orford, in this territory, by the *Sea Gull,* on her last trip down, have fallen victims to the barbarity of the savages. Several of them were from Portland, and all, we believe from this territory. These continued outrages cannot long fail to call down the vengeance of the whites upon the Indians of our southern frontier.

John M. Kirkpatrick returned to Portland somewhat worn, but very much alive on July 11 — according to Dodge. But his return was obviously earlier because his letter, recounting the events at Port Orford to the editor of the *Statesman* (at that time a weekly paper published in Oregon City,) is dated one day earlier.

Now over one hundred years later, accounts of the incident at Battle Rock have appeared in many books, magazines and newspapers. It depends upon the "thrust" the particular writer has in mind for his story, as well as how much red pencil an editor takes to it, as to how much of the original detail survives. The first variation following Kirkpatrick's *Statesman* explanation—written just thirty days after the fact—I have seen, shows up in Bancroft (1888) followed by Dodge (1898). Gaston offers another variant in his *Centennial History of Oregon* (Vol. I) in 1912. A recent account by Dorothy and Jack Sutton is in their *Indian Wars of the Rogue River* written for the Josephine County Historical Society in 1969.

Kirkpatrick's *Statesman* letter, set in 6-point type, occupies thirty-three column inches. Just setting the type one letter at a time by hand, was a real task and to allow this much space is an indication of the importance of the story at that time.

Among the differences noted on five details selected, each of the details appearing in at least two of the references chosen, *Statesman,* Bancroft, Dodge and Sutton, are these:

ITEM	*STATESMAN*	BANCROFT	DODGE	SUTTON
Cannon: Distance to Indians when fired	6 feet	Not stated. Indians and whites were in hand-to hand scuffle	8 feet	(Same as Bancroft)
Battle duration	15 minutes	15 minutes	Not stated	Not stated
Indians Killed by cannon	"some six or eight"	"several"	"12 or 13"	Shot caused "vacancy in crowd"
Final death toll of Indians	13	20	17	Not stated
Number of Indians who broke into camp for hand-to-hand fighting	3	1	2	Not stated

★　★　★　★　★

Gaston, Dodge and Sutton all use the picture Dodge labels to be that of John M. Kirkpatrick which the Kirkpatrick descendants consulted all disclaim.

Dodge and Gaston record the names of the nine men. But visitors hiking to the top of Battle Rock will probably step on a grave marker set into the narrow path on which the engraved name, at first look, does not seem familiar: SUMMERS, RALPH E. (JAKE). (I was told that although authorities allowed the marker to stay on the rock, the remains were removed some years ago.) Why these historians called "Jake" Summers by his middle name, Erastus, will probably never be known.

John M. Kirkpatrick died in Dunsmuir, California, in 1910, at the age of eighty-five. For some time he had made his home there with a son, Charles, after the death of his beloved "Becky" in 1904. They had been married forty-seven years.

Kirkpatrick is buried in the Odd Fellows Cemetary in Central Point, in Oregon's famous pear-growing Rogue Valley, alongside his youngest son, Willis. Except for a temporary stake placed in 1910 by an undertaker, there was no headstone until the summer of 1971.

Eyelyne Michael was instrumental in having the federal government provide a marker on the basis that her great-great-grandfather was a veteran. But after the various clerks and at least one "volunteer" finished the paper work, the marker was delivered to Central Point with the line "Mexican War" instead of "Cayuse Indian War."

The I.O.O.F. Cemetary in Central Point is not a perpetual care establishment. The sexton, Francis Marshall, a watch repairman in Central Point, told me there has been vandalism in the unkept cemetary and that records are incomplete. He escorted me to a plot and announced, "By deduction we are sure the two Kirkpatricks are in this plot but there is no way to tell which of the two graves is which." There is no marker for Willis.

The new bronze plate for "The Hero of Battle Rock," mounted in a two inch thick concrete slab, rests on top of sun-parched weeds and is visited regularly by a few crickets, grasshoppers, and an occasional field mouse.

Tile page from 1904 booklet
reduced from 4⅛ x 7¼ orginal.

I wish to thank the Kirkpatrick descendants previously named for their interest and helpfulness and for the use of some of their material.

It would be unseemly for me not to acknowledge that Francis Marshall left his business to escort me to the Central Point cemetery as I would never have found the J.M.K. marker without him.

I am indebted to the Board of Directors of the Coos-Curry Pioneer and Historical Association and especially to their curator, Dorice K. Baer, for letters and discussions that led to permission to quote from their material.

To Miss Eloise Ebert, the State Librarian of Oregon and her staff for isolating pertinent material for me and for the loan of *Statesman* microfilm, I take a bow.

The reproduction of the cover from the 1904 booklet was obtained through the courtesy of Larry Kirkpatrick. He received it originally from the library of the

University of Oregon, Eugene.

Let me never forget Dick Portal, Head Reference Librarian in Medford, Oregon, who handled inter-library loan arrangements and many professional chores that only other librarians know to appreciate.

Bert Webber
Medford, Oregon
December, 1973

REMARKS AND ACKNOWLEDGEMENTS FOR THE 1978 EXPANDED EDITION

I do not know of any writer or publisher who is not gratified to observe that his work is accepted to the point where additional printings are required. So it was with the 1973 printing which had to be repeated in 1974. Both printings were relatively small for we believed from the onset that the book would only have a limited demand. But we guessed wrong twice. The second printing also sold out within a few months. But committments of the publisher did not permit additional printings of *The Hero of Battle Rock*. A few remainder copies that came back from dealers were all sent to the Curry County Historical Society in Gold Beach, Oregon, just a few miles from Port Orford and Battle Rock.

By the summer of 1976, the number of requests for the book were being heard with increasing frequency particularly from librarians. After consultation, it was decided to bring back the book in an Expanded Edition. But how can one add to such a classic without diluting the original literature?

Since the writer is aquainted with photography, it was decided to improve the photographs which had been added to the 1973 printing and add more of them. (There were no pictures in the 1904 booklet. *See:* "Preface to 1973 Edition.") Thus, by illustrating the original work, we would create an Expanded Edition.

Many people have indicated interest in how a book like *The Hero of Battle Rock* is reprinted. The steps can be simple or complicated depending upon the circumstances. In this instance, the text of the 1904 original was sent, under contract, to a Taiwan firm for photo-offset reproduction. In due time the printed sheets were delivered to Ye Galleon Press in Fairfield, Washington. Before the sheets were assembled and a plain type cover printed, the writer, in cooperation with Glen Adams, Ye Galleon publisher, produced the pictures and the introductory pages for the 1973 edition. Those pages were printed on an LSB Harris offset press, now belonging to Ye Galleon Press but then installed in a shop in Moses Lake, Washington. When this portion of the work was completed, Adams printed the two-color title page on a Chandler & Price single sheet fed letter press in the Ye Galleon Fairfield shop.

The 1978 Expanded Edition reproduces the original text which has been completely reset on a Compugraphic 48 photo typesetter. To be faithful to the original work, the style, punctuation and spelling has been retained.

In the "Preface to the 1973 edition," the writer inserted a parenthetical about the body buried atop Battle Rock: "(I was told that although authorities allowed the marker to stay on the rock, the remains were removed some years ago.)" Since that was written we have learned more about that grave. It appears that the "removal" was not *from* the rock, but from a private grave on the property of Jake Summers *to* the present site on top of Battle Rock.

Jake Summers (right).
Volunteers removed remains of Summers from home plot to be reinterred with his wife and one son on top of Battle Rock.

Researchers conclude that the re-burial was during administration of Governor I.L. Paterson (Jan. 10, 1927——Dec. 21, 1930) but exact date is elusive.

Walt Schroeder, Oregon State University Extension Agent, and member of the Board of Directors of the Curry County Historical Society, was able to borrow the original set of snapshots of the reinterment from the Archieves of the City of Port Orford. These pictures were microfilmed in the writer's Medford photo lab and appear in print for the first time in the 1977 Expanded Edition. Unfortunately, we have been unable to learn when the reburial occurred for the date and name of the newspaper where the item appeared are both missing from the clipping. A number of photographs of early Port Orford are on display in the City Hall there. Some of these were chosen, with the help of City Hall personnel, for the present volume. Their assistance is appreciated. Many relics, photographs, and other matter from Port Orford, and from the rest of Curry County, are on display in the Curry County Museum. The museum is open daily in summer and on restricted hours in winter.

I am indebted to two members of the Curry County Historical Society who searched for, then loaned early pictures of Port Orford. Walt Schroeder has already been named. To him and to Edith Wakeman Jones I say, Thank You.

Contemporary photographs of Port Orford and Battle Rock are by the writer. Most of the pictures of early day views are on 35mm microfilm made by the writer with photolab assistance by son Dale B. Webber. Another son, Lauren T.

The hauling of the casket up the steep, rough, rocky end of Battle Rock was probably as arduous in the late 1920's as was the hauling of the cannon up the same route in 1851.

Webber, actively assisted on field trips particularly to Port Orford and to the top of Battle Rock. I thank both of them not only for their help but for their interest in working on an exciting chapter in Oregon's history.

Little is known of the lives of all of the men who stood before the attacking Indians on Battle Rock. As Kirkpatrick points out at the end of his narrative, Palmer, who was shot in the neck with an arrow obviously recovered for he became a wealthy saloon keeper in Salem. Slater was killed by Indians a few years later on the Rogue River. Summers farmed near Port Orford, and as has been pointed out is buried on top of Battle Rock. Ridoubt, who had been shot in the breast by an arrow was able to walk out of their entrapment but no further word about him seems available. Other than Kirkpatrick, only one of the men appears to have broken into print: Hedden.

Following the venture with Colonel T'Vault, Cyrus Hedden settled at Scottsburg. He opened a General Store at Scottsburg which he and his family operated for many years. When it was decided to close the business, they locked the doors on an extensive inventory of Patent Medicines. James Seeley White, a Portland writer, obtained access to the store where he photographed these old bottles with the medicines still in them. With the help of major drug firms, White researched the bottles and the medicines then wrote a book about Hedden and his

Researcher Bert Webber photographs marker for "Jake" Summers, his wife "Betsy" and one son for this book. Port Orford Chamber of Commerce set and dedicated the stone in 1953. Site is atop Battle Rock at Battle Rock State Wayside.

store titled, *Hedden's Store Handbook of Proprietory Medicines.* (Pacific Northwest Books P.O. Box 314, Medford, Oregon 97501. Cloth $6.75. Paper $3.00. Plus 50 cents shipping for either edition.) In the Introduction to his book, White establishes Hedden's earlier experience with the Indians on Battle Rock.

The Reference Department, Jackson County Library System, Medford, headed by Karen Chase, meticulously searched for data to make this Expanded Edition worthy of becoming a library reference tool itself. This professional as well as friendly help is cheerfully acknowledged.

Bert Webber
Central Point, Oregon
October 1977

The author is sensible that there are some typographical and other errors in the following work; but as they will be found **few** *and* **inconsiderable**, *it is not deemed worthwhile to notice them.*
—*Estwick Evans, 1819.*

Claimed to be the "First Photo Taken on Front Street, Portland, 1852," scene would have been about the same when Capt. Tichenor recruited nine men to be advance party for future City of Port Orford in May 1851.

THE HERO OF BATTLE ROCK

"I was working in Portland, Oregon, at the carpenter trade along in the latter part of May, 1851, when a friend by the name of Palmer, introduced me to Capt. Wm. Tichenor, who was at that time running an old steam propeller called the Sea Gull, between Portland, Oregon, and San Francisco, California. Before introducing me to Capt. Tichenor, my friend told me that the Capt. wanted eight or ten men to go down on the steamer with him to a place called Port Orford on the southwest coast of Oregon, where he intended to make a settlement, lay out a town, and build a road into the gold diggings in Southern Oregon and that all who went down with him should have a share in the town he and his partners were going to build. His partners were Mr. Hubboard, purser on the Sea Gull, and the Hon. Butler King, then chief in the Custom House in San Francisco. After I made the acquaintance

17

Capt. William Tichenor in later years. When he planned the City of Port Orford he was apparently unaware of possible trouble with Indians. In 1851 he left Kirkpatrick and eight others as an advance party to start the town, but they were routed by Indians.

of Captain Tichenor he painted the whole enterprise in such glowing colors that I was really infatuated with the prospect. He told me that there was not a particle of danger from the Indians, that he had been ashore among them many times and they were perfectly friendly, so I went to work to hunt up a party to go down with us on the Sea Gull.

I gathered together eight young men who were willing to go down on the trip. Their names were J.H. Eagan, John T. Slater, George Riboubt, T.D. Palmer, Joseph Hussey, Cyrus W. Hedden, James Carigan, Erastus Summers and myself, making nine in all. Captain Tichenor agreed to furnish us arms, ammunition and supplies, and take us down on his steamer. He told us all to get ready to go as he would sail from Portland on the 4th of June, 1851.

We were ready and sailed from Portland on time. On the 5th we arrived in Astoria. I had been selected by the party as the captain of the expedition so I went to Captain Tichenor and told him I wanted to see the arms he was going to furnish us to defend ourselves with in case we had to fight. "Oh," he said, "there is no danger from the Indians." We then told him that we would go no further unless he furnished us with arms to defend ourselves. He then went ashore, and bought, at a junk shop, three old flint lock muskets, one old sword that was half eaten with rust

J.H. Egan, one of the defenders of Battle Rock.

and a few pounds of lead and three or four pounds of powder. We told him that he had certainly brought us a hard looking outfit of arms to fight Indians with. "You will never need them," said he, "but having them will make you look dangerous anyway." Just then a young officer from Fort George stepped up to me and told me he had a very good United States rifle he would let me have at cost, viz: $20. I went ashore with him and bought the rifle and also some ammunition. It proved to be a magnificent shooting gun. Our entire armament consisted now of one U.S. rifle, belonging to myself, one six shooting rifle belonging to Carigan, three old flint lock muskets, one old sword, one fine shooting revolver 38 cal., one pair of deringers loaned to me by a friend in Portland for the trip, about five pounds of rifle powder and ten pounds of bar lead. This constituted our entire outfit to defend ourselves with when we left Astoria on the evening of the 6th of June 1851. On the morning of the 9th we were landed on the beach just below Battle Rock. There were a few Indians in sight who appeared friendly, but I could see that they did not like to have us there. I told Captain Tichenor that I did not like the looks of things at all and those Indians meant mischief. There was one thing more that we wanted and that was the old cannon Captain Tichenor had on board the Sea Gull. He laughed at us at first for wanting it, but when we told him we would not stay without it he studied a little bit and then said all right he would send it ashore. He

Probably the earliest drawing to be published of the village of Port Orford. *Harper's Weekly* used it on page 590 of their October 1856 issue. Battle Rock on left.

sent his mate with one of my men, Eagan, who was an old man-of-wars man, back to the steamer for the gun. They soon returned bringing the cannon and copper magazine that contained three or four cartridges each holding two pounds of powder. As soon as the cannon arrived the Captain bid us good bye and left for San Francisco, saying he would return in fourteen days and bring a better supply of arms and more men to aid him in his enterprise. After he left we lost no time in making our camp on what was to be called Battle Rock as long as Oregon has a history. We hauled the old cannon to the top of the rock and placed it so as to command the narrow ridge where the Indians would have to crowd together before they could get to the top of the rock where we were camped.

About half way up to the top of the rock there was a bench of nearly level ground about thirty feet wide, from that to the top of the rock the ridge was quite narrow. After getting the gun in place, Eagan and I went to work to load it and get ready for the fight that I felt was coming. We put in a two pound sack of powder and on top of that about half of an old cotton shirt and then on top of that as much bar lead cup up in pieces of from one to two inches in length as I could hold in my two hands, than a couple of old newspapers on top. We then primed the gun with some fine rifle powder and trained it so as to rake the narrow ridge in front of the muzzle and the gun was ready for business. We cleaned up all our other arms and

Earliest known photograph of Battle Rock (above) made about 1912. Observe few trees on top, no driftwood in front of rock. Compare with pictures on pages 35 and 47.

loaded them ready for use. Just as soon as the Indians saw the steamer going away without us they appeared very cross and ordered us away, making signs to us that they would kill us if we did not go. Then they left for their camps down the beach. On the morning of the 10th they were back again in larger numbers and shooting arrows at us from too great a distance to do us any damage. About 9 o'clock a large canoe, containing twelve warriors, came up the coast from the direction of the mouth of Rogue River. Among them was one tall fellow wearing a red shirt who seemed to be their leader. As soon as the canoe touched the sand they all jumped out and carried it out on the beach. The fellow in the red shirt drew a long knife, waved it over his head, gave a terrible yell and, with at least one hundred of his braves, started for us with a rush. I stood by the gun holding a piece of tarred rope with one end in the fire ready, as soon as the Indians crowded on the narrow ridge in front of the cannon to let them have the contents when it would do the most execution. The air was full of arrows coming from at least a hundred bows. James Carigan had picked up a pine board about 15 inches wide, 8 feet long and 1.3 inches in thickness. He stood right behind me and held the board in front of us both. thirty-seven arrows hit the board and at least half of them showed the points through it. Two of my men were disabled. Palmer was shot through the neck and was bleeding badly; Ridoubt was shot in the breast, the arrow sticking into the

21

Artist drew picture based on Kirkpatrick's report. Note defenders holding large board in which are imbedded many arrows.

breast bone, making a painful wound, and Slater ran and laid down in a hole behind the tent. This left six of us to fight it out with the Indians who still kept coming. When they were crowded on the narrow ridge, the red shirted fellow in the lead and not more than eight feet from the muzzle of the gun, I applied the fiery end of the rope to the priming. The execution was fearful, at least twelve or thirteen men were killed outright and such a tumbling of scared Indians I never saw before or since. The gun was upset by the recoil; but we never stopped for that but rushed out to them and soon cleared the rock of all the live warriors. We counted seventeen dead Indians on the rock and this was the bloody baptism that gave the name of Battle Rock to our old camp at Port Orford on the 10th day of June, 1851.

Some incidents that occurred during the battle are worth relating. There were two warriors who passed the crowd and were not hit by any of the slugs of lead fired from the cannon. One of these, a big strong looking Indian, made up his mind that he wanted my scalp; as soon as the cannon was fired he rushed to me with a big knife. Carigan shot him in the shoulder and Summers shot him through the bowels and still he came on. He made a lick at me with his knife, which I knocked

"How a small canon (*sic*) done its work."

out his hand with my left, when he grabbed for his knife I pulled one of the deringers from my pocket and shot him in the head, the ball going in at one temple and out at the other. He turned then and ran twenty feet and fell dead among the Indians that were killed by the cannon. The other Indian went for Eagan whose musket missed fire, as the Indian was in the act of fixing an arrow in his bow, when Eagan hit him over the head with the barrel of his musket bending it more than six inches. The blow stunned the Indian and as quick as lightening Eagan jumped at him and took his bow away, he then jumped back and turned his musket and gave him three or four blows with the butt knocking him entirely off the rock into the ocean.

After the fight was all over probably an hour, an Indian chief came up the beach within hailing distance and laid down his bow, quiver of arrows and knife and then stepped forward and made signs that he wanted to come to our camp. I went down to the beach and met him and brought him up to the camp. He was by all odds the finest specimen of physical manhood that I ever looked at. He made signs to us that he wanted to carry away the dead Indians. I made him understand that he could bring another Indian to help him. He called out for one more to come up to the camp. They would take the dead ones on their back, pack them down from where they lay, across the narrow sandy beach and up a steep trail

23

Snags, left from the devastating forest fire of 1868 which burned
down all but three of the village buildings, seen in background.

toward the north and over a ridge and out of sight. They did this eight times, and
where they laid the dead was over three hundred yards from our camp. Some of
the Indians were quite large, several of them weighing over two hundred pounds.
As a feat of strength and endurance it was simply wonderful. They carried away all
the dead except the fellow who wore the red shirt. I tried to get the big chief to
carry him off but he shook his head and stooped down and tore his shirt in two and
then gave him a kick with his foot and turned and walked away. We had to drag
the fellow afterwards and bury him in the sand. We all remarked that he was very
white for an Indian, he had yellow hair and a freckled face. I pronounced him to
be a white man. He turned out to be a white man who had been among the
Indians for many years, they having saved him from the wreck of a Russian ship
that was lost on the Oregon coast many years ago.

Another incident of our day's battle was this: After the Indian chief and his
man had carried away all of the dead warriors we went to work to make a
breastwork on each side of our gun, this was to make it a little more difficult for
the Indians to get into our camp, I was standing outside on the narrow ridge in

24

Port Orford looking south about 1900. Road over Cemetery Hill in right, high center.

front of our gun watching some Indians who were about three hundred yards away. I was leaning on my rifle when Joe Hussey came out of the camp and laid his right hand on my left shoulder, I turned my head to see what he wanted when spat a bullet hit his thumb cutting it about half off. This was the first rifle shot we had heard from the Indians since the fight began. The Indian with the gun had crawled down unnoticed by us, into a large pile of rocks about sixty yards away from where I stood when he shot. He was so sure that he had hit me that he jumped out from the rocks and showed himself; then it was my turn. I had a slug ball and five buck-shot in my rifle and in an instant I drew a head on him and when my gun cracked he jumped three feet into the air and fell dead. Eagan said, "I am going after his gun." I told him to hold on until I had loaded my rifle for, says I, "There may be other Indians in the rocks and I want to be ready." As soon as my gun was loaded he ran down and picked up the gun and seeing it was of no account he broke the stock and came back bringing the Indians head dress with him. It was made of sea shells of different colors and was quite pretty. He said the bullet from my rifle had broken his right arm and passed through his body and cut

Louis Knapp built a hotel about 1867 but during the forest fire in October 1868 the hotel, and most all of the town, was destroyed when the fire swept to the edge of the beach. Knapp rebuilt on a new site in 1883 and had about twenty rooms, including private quarters for his family. He and his wife kept a lighted lamp in a window facing the sea as a warning to ships of the dangerous coastline. The Knapp's were hospitable and their light attracted shipwrecked sailors and others stranded on the lonely rugged coast. Eventually some of the rooms were given famous names. (One of the prominent library reference works states that the rooms were named for famous visitors who slept in them including Jack London, Joe Meek, W.H. Seward "[who] stopped on his way to ...Alaska," and others. However Louis L. Knapp, a son, told a researcher of the Curry County Historical Society in 1977 that the names were given to the rooms as a publicity venture and had no bearing on who stayed in the hotel.) The Knapp Hotel served the south Oregon coast with distinction until it was finally torn down after World War II because the realignment for the present Oregon Coast Highway (U.S. 101) went through the building. Plans called for the hotel to be dismantled. When workmen started, they discovered that it had been constructed by a ship's carpenter and was so tight that it was impossible to take it apart for salvage. Accordingly, the building was razed. The hotel was just south of Battle Rock State Wayside Historical Marker. The main door of the hotel would be on the center line of the highway.

Port Orford between 1905-1910.

his left hand entirely off. He never knew what hurt him. This was the last Indian killed by us in our first day's battle. We could only count twenty Indians that we had killed; but years afterward we learned from the Indians that there were twenty-three killed.

In our talk with the big chief we made him understand that in fourteen days more the steamer would return and take us away and for fourteen days we were not molested by them, in fact we never saw an Indian; but on the morning of the 15th they were there in force, some three or four hundred of them in their war paint. They evidently meant business now as we had lied to them, the steamer did not arrive as we had promised them and we could not make them understand why the vessel did not come. Two or three hundred warriors were going through with a regular war dance on the beach and every time they would turn around so as to face us they would snap their bow strings at us and make signs that they would soon have our scalps. The big chief was now their leader. He had his warriors all drawn up around him about two hundred and fifty yards from us. He made a speech to them so loud that we could hear every word he said above the roar of the surf and he did some of the finest acting that I ever saw before or since. When he stopped talking he drew a long knife and waved it around his head, gave a terrible yell and started for us followed by not less than three hundred warriors. I had called to my side James Carrigan who was the best rifle shot of any of my men. I told him to

27

Port Orford about 1921. Chas. Long Grocery Store on left.
Gilling's Hardware Store on right.

take a good rest, draw his lungs full of air, keep cool and wait until they came near enough so as to be sure and kill the leader, for it was either the big chief or us who must go. When he got within about one hundred yards of us I raised my rifle to my shoulder and said, "Fire!" We both fired at the same time and down he dropped, we had both hit him in the breast and one of our bullets had gone through his heart, killing him instantly. Had a hundred thunder bolts dropped among his warriors they could not have stopped them as suddenly as killing their big chief. They gathered around his body and with a groan that was terrible, picked him up and carried him away to the north out of sight. In about an hour another great tall fellow wearing an old red shirt, came up the beach and commenced calling the Indians around him. He soon collected a couple of hundred warriors about him and made a speech to them 'about five minutes in length. We could see by his frantic gestures and talk that he was urging the Indians to rush on us and wipe us out. When he stopped talking he waved his big knife over his head and started for us, pointing his knife at us and motioning that our heads must be cut off. We were ready for him and when he came close to where the other chief was killed, we fired and he dropped dead. This ended all efforts on the part of their chiefs to induce the Indians to rush on us. They had had enough of that kind of business. They drew back to the edge of the woods, about three hundred yards away from our camp, and had a big talk, after which they commenced going down the beach to a place a little over a mile from our camp, where there were a number of fires burning. We could see a number of canoes loaded with Indians coming up from the direction of the mouth of Rogue River and landing near these fires. They were evidently concentrating their forces for a night attack on us. We had now taken note of our situation. We we *(sic)* [were] surrounded on one side by thousands of miles of

28

Port Orford about 1925. Camera faces south. Compare with picture on page 32.

water and on the other side by at least four or five hundred hostile Indians and one hundred and fifty miles or more from any settlement of white men. We had also taken stock of our ammunition and had little left. About six loads apiece for our rifles. Something had to be done and that before night, for if they made a night attack on us we could not possibly stand them off, so I told the boys that if we could gain the woods and they would stand by me I would take them all through to the settlements. We made up our minds that it was the only chance to save our scalps. We were still watched by ten or twelve Indians not more than two hundred yards away. To get rid of those fellows so that we could gain the woods was the next question we had to solve. "Now," said I, "If they contemplate a night attack on us we must convince those fellows on watch that we have no notion of going away." We all went to work as hard as we could to strengthen our breastwork. We cut down one of the pine trees that grew on Battle Rock, cut off the limbs and piled them on top of our breastworks. As soon as the Indians, who were on watch, saw what we were doing they were sure we were determined to stay. They then started down the beach to join the others. We counted them as they got up out of the grass, and there were one hundred and fourteen. I will say that I never, in all my experience with Indians before or since, saw as fine a body of warriors as those. We were now pretty sure that they had all left, but Eagan climbed up to the top of one of the trees and looked in every direction but could see no sign of any Indians

Port Orford from the air probably in the 1930's. Battle Rock at top to left of center.

except down the beach where they were having a grand war dance. Now was our chance. We left everything we had in camp; our two tents, our blankets and what little provisions we had, and with nothing but our guns and an ax and all the small ropes we had, with two or three sea biscuits apiece, we bid farewell to our old camp on Battle Rock, and started on our fearful retreat through an unknown country. It was now about 4 o'clock in the afternoon. We had determined to keep as near the beach as possible. We travelled with all our might to get as far as we could before night overtook us. When we were about three miles from Port Orford just as we were going around a point of rocks on an old trail, we met about thirty Indian wariors fully armed, going down to join the others. We raised a yell and charged right at them. We never fired a shot, but they ran like scared wolves. We kept right

Wide paved street awaits developer's interest in Port Orford in spring of 1977.

on and just between sunset and dark we came to quite a river and, as good luck would have it, we struck this stream just at the turn of the tide so that by wading out on the bar a little way we were able to get across without any trouble. Fifteen minutes later we would have had to build a raft to cross on. This stream was not down on any map that I had ever seen at that time. I think it is now called Elk River. After crossing this stream we struck into the woods and travelled all night, guiding our steps by the roar of the surf breaking on the rocks. There was no time to lose. We knew that the Indians would follow us so we traveled on as hard as we could, wading streams of water, some of considerable size, and making our way through a dense growth of timber and brush. About 3 o'clock the next day we came to the edge of what seemed to us a large plain. It looked to be miles in extent and was covered with a heavy growth of high grass and proved to be an immense swamp.

We now determined to try and cross this swamp and reach the sea after dark and travel all night. We floundered around in this swamp all night, sometimes in water up to our armpits, until after dark when we found a little island of about an acre of dry land and covered with a thick growth of small fir bushes. Here we laid down and tried to rest and sleep but encountered a new enemy in the shape of clouds of mosquitoes. There was no escape from them and they were the hungriest lot that I had ever seen. In the morning, as soon as it was light enough for us to see our way out, we struck for the beach again and in about an hour we reached an Indian trail fully twenty feet wide where hundreds of Indians had gone. They were now ahead of us. We followed on their trail a few miles when we came to a stream

31

Seldom is the day when the wind does not blow at Port Orford.
1977. Compare with picture on page 29.

of water about four rods wide and two feet deep. Here the trail turned up this stream and left the beach. We at once came to the conclusion that the Indians had followed us that far the first night and when daylight came they had found that we had not traveled on the beach, so they struck up this stream, thinking of intercepting us when we reached this stream on our way. We crossed on the beach and were now ahead of the Indians. We now put in our best time traveling as hard as we could. About five o'clock we reached the mouth of the Coquille River where we were confronted by a large stream of water and on the opposite side of the river were three or four hundred Indians all drawn up in line of battle ready to prevent our crossing. They were making signs that they would kill us if we attempted to cross, so there was now no alternative but to keep up on the south side of the river and do our best to prevent coming into collision with these Indians that were so numerous and hostile. We now came to the conclusion that we had better try and cross the mountains and strike the wagon road that led from the settlements in Oregon down to California. About three or four miles from the mouth of the Coquille River, on the south side, rises quite a high mountain, so we determined to go to the top of this mountain in order to study the surrounding country. Three or four hundred Indians kept right opposite watching us, with nothing but the river between them and us. Just as we reached the foot of this mountain the Indians stopped a few minutes and divided their forces. One party of over one hundred turned off to the left and ran up a short ravine toward the north. They soon disappeared over a low pass to the left and went back toward their village at the mouth of the river. Their object was to get their canoes, cross the river, overtake us and kill or capture us. When we had ascended this mountain some distance we could see the Indians crossing the river in their canoes. We hurried on as fast as we could travel and between sun down and dark we reached the top of the mountain, tired, hungry and nearly worn out. Here we determined to rest and get some sleep. We worked our way into the thicket of brush where we found a kind of sink hole, about twenty feet in diameter and about three feet deep, covered on the bottom with a rank growth of grass with thick brush all around it. Here we all laid down and were soon fast asleep. Just as soon as it began to be light in the morning, notwithstanding there was a thick fog, we were up and off, traveling in a northeasterly direction as hard as we could. In about an hour we struck the river again at a point where the timber came down close to the water. We found a lot of dry drift wood and soon made a raft large enough to carry the three men who could not swim and our guns and the ballance of us swimming and pushing the raft ahead of us. The river at this point was about two hundred yards wide. When we reached the opposite bank and landed we supposed that we had crossed the river but we had only landed on an island and did not know it until we had taken all our ropes off of the raft and let the logs go. We had not gone more than three hundred yards when, to our consternation, we discovered that we had another branch of the river to cross nearly as wide as the one we had crossed. There was not a stick of timber on the island to make a raft out of, and as the fog was beginning to break away, there was not time to lose, so one of the men, George Ridoubt, volunteered to swim across with the ax and cut off a dry pine tree projected out over the water towards us. Our intention was to get the three men, who could not swim, on to the tree, let them bold our guns and the balance of us swim along and guide the tree. Just as the tree fell into the water three Indians came around the

Battle Rock. Note lack of driftwood in this undated view compared with huge deposit of driftwood in 1973 on page 35.

bend in a canoe. They were busy watching the man that was chopping and did not see us until they were close to us. We hailed them and made signs that we wanted them to land and take us over the river to where Ridoubt was.

This they refused to do, but when they saw three or four rifles leveled on them they concluded to come to where we were. We all piled into the canoe and they landed us on the main land just as the sun broke through the fog. We did not tarry long till we were on our weary tramp again. We were now very weak, not having eaten anything for three nights and four days. We saw plenty of game, but did not dare to fire a shot, for it would have brought at least three hundred Indians on to us in ten minutes, and they would have made short work of us. The men who were with me had no knowledge of woodcraft and but little of Indian warfare. They were on an average as brave a company of men as the same number that could be found. There was not one among them who could have taken the lead and kept a course without running around in a circle. When I found this out I saw that their lives as well as my own depended on my keeping in the lead. I had a good knowledge of woodcraft and could take a course and keep it as long as it was necessary. I had also some little knowledge of the cunning and trickery of the

Although referred to as "the cave," opening in the rock is a natural arch easily accessible at low tide from either side. South opening is at tide line in picture. In recent years driftwood has accumulated near the rock to the delight of beachcombers. *See:* Webber, Bert and Margie, *Beachcombing and Camping Along the Northwest Coast.* (Ye Galleon Press, Fairfield, Wash.)

Indians, having crossed the Rocky Mountains in company with Kit Carson; and I will here say that of all the men that I ever came in contact with or associated with Christopher Carson knew all the tricks and cunning of the Indians better than any man I ever saw. I hope you will not think me egotistical when I say that I felt equal to the task of leading my party through to a place of safety. After crossing this branch of the river we struck out in a northwesterly direction, through the timber, intending, if we could, to reach the beach by night, and then travel as hard as we could all night if necessary. We traveled on through the thick heavy timber until it got so dark that we could not get along, so we all laid down by the side of a big log and slept until daylight. We then jumped up and were off in the same direction we had been traveling the day before. In about an hour we emerged from the timber and soon got down to the beach. We struck the sea at a point where a long reef of rocks extended quite a ways out into the ocean. These rocks, near the shore, were covered with mussels which we broke from the rocks and commenced eating them

Wide path for walkers and bicycles (motor vehicles not permitted) from Battle Rock State Wayside to the beach in front of the rock. 1973. Observe end of small boat jetty in right rear.

raw. They soon made us sick, so we built a fire and began roasting them and that made them much better. We were eating our first lot of roasted mussels when one of the Indians, who had crossed us over the north branch of the Coquille river the day before, came down to us. As soon as he got near to us, he commenced talking Jargon. He said he had seen me in Portland, that he had kept right behind us in the woods after we left the river, and that he was afraid to come to us in the woods believing we would kill him. He said that the Indians were coming up on the beach from the mouth of the Coquille, and we must hurry as fast as we could. Each one of us took all the live mussels we could carry, but did not stop to cook them as we intended to roast them when we got to a place of safety. We now struck up the beach as fast as we could go, the Indian in the lead. We traveled on until about 3 o'clock in the afternoon when the Indian called our attention to a white pole about eight inches in diameter and twenty feet high, standing in a great pile of rocks at the edge of the beach. When we passed this pole and monument, the Indian said we were now safe, as the California Siwashes would not dare to come above that pole, for the Coos Bay, Umpqua, Clickatats, and some other tribes he mentioned, would make war on them and drive them back. After resting a little while we traveled on for about two hours and, turning into a little cove, we built up a fire and roasted our mussels and ate them. We then took up our line of march and

BATTLE ROCK STATE PARK

Battle Rock as viewed from public parking lot on Highway 101.

BATTLE ROCK STATE PARK HAS BEEN DEDICATED TO THOSE EXPLORERS AND PIONEERS WHO PREPARED THE WAY FOR THE SETTLEMENT OF THE SOUTHERN OREGON COAST. CAPTAIN GEORGE VANCOUVER SIGHTED AND DETERMINED THE LATITUDE OF CAPE BLANCO ON APRIL 24, 1792, NAMING IT CAPE ORFORD. THE ROADSTEAD WAS CHARTED IN 1860 BY WILLIAM P. MCARTHUR, COMMANDER OF THE U.S. COAST SURVEY VESSEL EWING, WHO CALLED IT EWING HARBOR BUT THE NAME PORT ORFORD HAS PERSISTED. CAPT. WILLIAM TICHENOR OF THE SHIP SEAGULL LANDED NINE MEN ON JUNE 9, 1851 FOR THE PURPOSE OF ESTABLISHING A SETTLEMENT. THE NEXT DAY THEY WERE ATTACKED BY INDIANS AND BESIEGED ON THE ISLAND NOW CALLED BATTLE ROCK. AFTER REPULSING THE INDIANS IN SEVERAL ASSAULTS THE PARTY ESCAPED TO THE UMPQUA SETTLEMENT. ON JULY 4, 1851 CAPT. TICHENOR AGAIN ARRIVED WITH A WELL-ARMED PARTY OF SIXTY-SEVEN MEN AND ESTABLISHED A BLOCK HOUSE AND THE SETTLEMENT OF WHICH HE BECAME A PERMANENT RESIDENT AFTER HIS RETIREMENT FROM THE SEA.

traveled till it was dark and then turned off to our right where we found some dry sand, in another little cove, and all laid down and slept until morning. As soon as it was daylight we were up and away. That afternoon we reached Coos Bay. The Indians met us more than a mile from their camp and brought us dried salmon, dried elk meat and salmon berries. They were extremely friendly and expressed

A 1975 view of Battle Rock, offshore rocks to the south and much driftwood.

themselves as being very glad that we had not been killed by the California Siwashes. We staid all night with these Indians who seemed to vie with each other in doing everything they could for us. In the morning they took us across the bay and landed us about where Empire City now stands. They told us that we would make the mouth of the Umpqua the next day. We bid our friends goodbye and struck across the sand hills and through swamps, where sometimes the water was three or four feet deep. We floundered around in these sand hills and swamps until we were nearly tired out and struck for the beach again. About an hour before dark we reached the beach. The wind was blowing so hard from the west that it made it difficult and unpleasant to travel against, so we left the beach and sought shelter behind some sand hills that raise to more than a hundred feet above the sea. We found some dry pine logs near a thicket of brush and soon had a big fire going. Here we laid down and slept until morning, notwithstanding we were soaked with the mist that had been driven across the sand hills by the gale in the night. After we

Battle Rock "cave." Inter-
tidal life (star fish, etc.)
can be found along the
rock walls. One can walk
through this natural arch
only at low tide.

had dried ourselves a little by our fire we struck out for the beach. The gale had subsided and the beach, for more than one hundred yards in width and as far as we could see up and down the beach, was literally covered with fish that had been driven ashore the night before by the gale. "Luck at last," cried Eagan, "Here is fish enough for a feast for the Gods;" and each one of us picked up two apiece, weighing 5 or 6 pounds each, and back we went to our camp where we had left a big bed of coals, where we roasted our fish, eating all we could of one and taking the rest with us. That afternoon we reached the mouth of the Umpqua River. The Indians on watch for us had notified the white men on the other side of the river that the white men, who had shot a keg of nails into the Indians at Port Orford, killing many of them, were on the other side of the river. We could see the white men launching their boats at what was called Umpqua City; at that time it consisted of one house built of sheet iron and one tent. In about an hour they had reached us and taken us aboard. Having a fair wind they hoisted sail and just as the sun was setting on the 2d day of July, 1851, we were landed and made welcome in

The Port Orford beach upon which Indians gathered for the attack on nine white men in 1851. 1973 view.

white men's quarters, after having an experience that not soon would we forget. Never did a set of poor, weary, ragged, hungry white men receive a more royal welcome than we did at the hands of Dr. Joseph Drew and his associates at their camp at the mouth of the Umpqua River. We rested there one day and on the morning of the 4th they took us in their boats and, having sailed up the river, they left us at another new town called Scottsburg. Here we landed about 1 o'clock and after I had eaten some dinner I bade farewell to my comrades and struck out for Portland. The rest were so worn out and footsore that they were compelled to lay by and rest. I traveled as hard as I could and on the night of the fourth I stayed with a man whose name was Wells. I left his house before daylight and, after a hard day's tramp, I reached the hospitable house of the grand old pioneer Jesse Applegate. He had just received his mail from Portland and was busy reading the account of our fight with the Indians. The conclusion drawn from the account was that we were killed and burned up. I did not interrupt him until he got through reading his paper. I then asked him if I could get some supper and a place to stay all night. "I can give you some supper but all my beds and blankets are in use," he said. I told him I was quite hungry and it made very little difference with me whether I had a bed or not as I had been sleeping for some time without a bed or

40

Most every community had a town band and Port Orford was no different. With the heavy brass: 4 cornets, 1 fluglehorn, 4 alto horns, 1 slide trombone, 2 baritones, 1 tuba and a brace of drums and cymbal, the two clarinetists must have had to play with great enthusiasm to be heard. Photo about 1915. (Right) Research assistant Lauren Webber—a musician—models antique bass drum which is on display in Port Orford City Hall.

blanket. He then commenced talking about those unfortunate young men that had been lured into the jaws of death by misrepresentation. "Why," said he, "those Indians down the coast, combined with their brothers, the Rogue River Indians, are the worst Indians on the American continent, and the bravest. Every old settler in Oregon knows that. The man or company that persuaded them to go down with the view of making a settlement at Port Orford was guilty of a great wrong." "Well," said I, "Mr. Applegate, I am happy to inform you that the men were not murdered but escaped, and eight of them I left at Scotsburg yesterday and I am

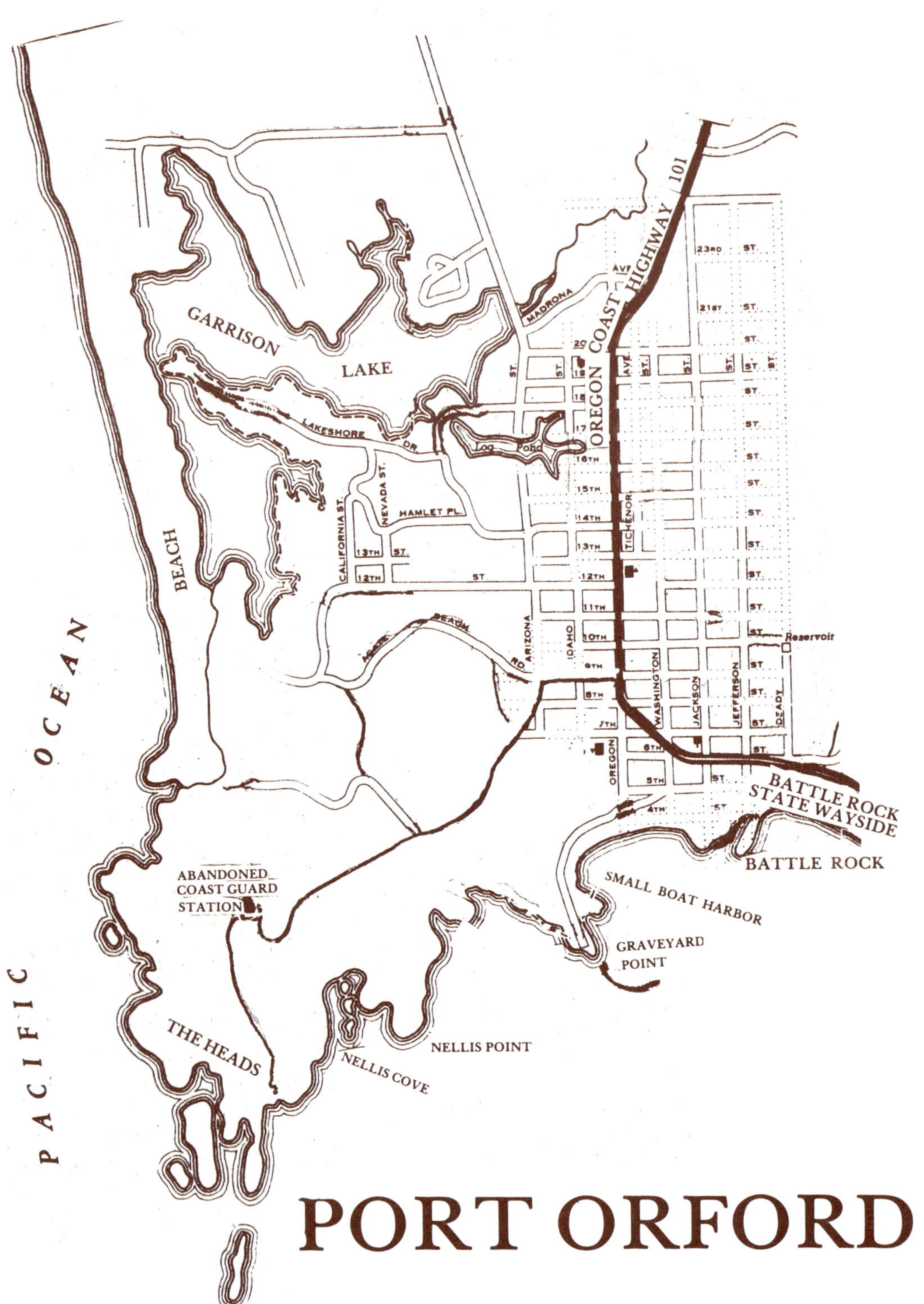

OCEAN
PACIFIC
BEACH
GARRISON LAKE
LAKESHORE DR.
Log Pond
CALIFORNIA ST.
NEVADA ST.
HAMLET PL.
13TH ST.
12TH
BEACH RD.
ARIZONA
IDAHO
MADRONA
OREGON COAST HIGHWAY 101
23RD ST.
21ST ST.
ST.
20 ST.
19 ST.
18
17
16TH
15TH
14TH
13TH
12TH
11TH
10TH
9TH
8TH
7TH
6TH
5TH
4TH
ST.
ST.
ST.
ST.
ST.
ST.
ST.
ST.
ST.
ST.
ST.
ST.
ST.
ST.
ST.
ST.
AVE.
TICHENOR
WASHINGTON
JACKSON
JEFFERSON
DEADY
OREGON
Reservoir
BATTLE ROCK STATE WAYSIDE
BATTLE ROCK
SMALL BOAT HARBOR
GRAVEYARD POINT
ABANDONED COAST GUARD STATION
THE HEADS
NELLIS COVE
NELLIS POINT

PORT ORFORD

PORT ORFORD

Aerial Photo of October 2, 1971.

Port Orford Small Boat Basin in 1977.

the ninth." I told him my name and then I gave him an account of our retreat and his remark was, after I got through, "Wonderful, wonderful."

Here I must make an explanation. I had written a full account of our first battle with the Indians on Battle Rock and also an account of our last battle, fifteen days afterward, and closed the account with these words, "We are now surrounded by three or four hundred Indians hungry for our scalps, on one side; by thousands of miles of water on the other; and at least 150 miles from any white man's house. We have but little grub and are nearly out of ammunition and if the Indians should make a night attack and rush on us we certainly could not defend ourselves against so many." This paper I folded up and placed in the back of an old book, went to the stump of the pine tree that we had just cut down, and buried the book in a hole about a foot deep, then scraped off the bark on one side of the stump, just over where the book was, and wrote with a piece of red chalk these two words, "Look beneath."

When the steamer Sea Gull reached San Francisco, after leaving us at Port Orford, she was embargoed for debt and tied up, so it was impossible for Captain Tichenor to return in fourteen days as he had promised. Col. John B. Ferguson, then U.S. mail agent for California and Oregon, and a friend of mine, learning

A power hoist lifts a fishing boat from the water and places it on a dolly which is rolled to a "parking" space on the wharf. Boats "parked" in lee of hill, out of the wind and winter storm-tossed water receive less damage than if left at anchor in the basin.   1977.

from Captain Tichenor that he was tied up for debt and could not return on time, and knowing much more about the Indians on the coast than the captain did, went to the captain of the steamer Columbia and dispatched him one day before her regular sailing time, with strict orders to call at Port Orford and take us back to Portland. The steamer stopped at Port Orford the day after we left Battle Rock. The captain and a number of passengers went ashore and found the body of the fellow in the red shirt that we had killed in the first fight and buried in the sand, but the tide had washed him out and he was then as white as could be. They made sure that it was one of us when they went up on the rock where everything showed evidence of a fight. In looking around their attention was called to the words written on the stump and they soon dug up the book and after reading it they were sure that the Indians had wiped us out. As no Indians were to be seen, they concluded to search a little further for more evidence of our fate. They finally found where the big fire had been built and in some of the ashes they found some human teeth and some charred pieces of human bones. This ended their search as they were now sure that we had been killed and burned. What they really found was where the Indians had burned their dead after the first battle with us. They then returned to the steamer in the full belief that we had all been killed and burned, all but the body they found on the beach.

The steamer sailed at once with the account of our trouble up to the time we left Battle Rock. This was published in the Oregonian as soon as possible, and this was the account that Applegate was reading when I reached his house. Nearly all my friends in Portland and all over Oregon really believed that it was all up with me and all my party. Not so with the old mountaineers, Joe Meek, Otway and Wilks. They all said that we would turn up all right yet, and when I reached Portland with the news that my party was all safe they were as happy as man could

"Port Orford Jakie" (pron: jaykee) is alledged to have been the last of
the Cos-utt-hen-tun band of Indians who had their main village just
south of Humbug Mountain. Since he was the last Indian around the
people of Port Orford adopted him, dressed him for their parades and
called him "chief" which he dearly loved. There is evidence that Jakie
witnessed the massacre on Battle Rock when he was about eight. In later
years he thrilled youngsters by telling about it. The late Minnie King
Jolly, of Port Orford, recalled one of these story telling sessions in 1904
when "chief" was in his sixties. She told the compiler. "He acted out his
parts with dance. He was the pet of the local children—a great teller of
Indian lore." "Chief" Jakie was also awarded a land grant. He died
about 1906. The picture is from an oil portrait by Minnie King Jolly
done from memory about 1958.

be. I reached my old quarters in Portland on the 11th day of July, 1851, strong and
rugged, having had enough of adventure to do me for one time.

As to my comrades on this expedition, I never saw but two of them
afterwards. Eagan settled in Portland, married, raised a family. Palmer settled in
Salem, had a saloon and was quite well fixed. These two men I saw quite often. In
1866 Slater was killed by Indians, on Rogue River. In 1855 Cy. Hedden joined a
company under Colonel T'Vault and tried to reach Port Orford by land. T'Vault's
party consisted of ten or twelve men and when they reached the Coquille River,
Hedden pointed out our trail to T'Vault and told him he was on dangerous ground
and must be cautious. He paid no attention to Hedden's warning, but went into
camp on a grassy plat not far from where he crossed the river. In the night the
Indians surprised his camp, killing the most of his men. Hedden escaped with a
man by the name of Williams, who had been wounded with an arrow, and when
the shaft was pulled out the head was left in his body. Hedden and Williams finally
reached Scottsburg where Williams suffered for months but the arrow point finally
worked itself out. Hedden stayed and waited on him until he got well.

When I look back over this whole affair I think you will agree with me that,
take it all in all, the history of the Port Orford expedition is worthy of a place in the
history of the early settlements. As to our fight, considering our inexperience and
the arms we had, we certainly did well. There is no other battle in Indian warfare
that I know of, that equals it, except that most glorious defense Mrs. Harris made

---

The "Mrs. Harris" refers to Indian trouble in the Rogue Valley. She was rescued by a posse of volunteers which had
assembled at Jacksonville for that purpose. *See:* "Massacre of Oct. 9, 1855" in Walling, A.G. *History of Southern
Oregon* p. 246.

The number of lumber mills along streams which empty into the Pacific Ocean along the Northwest Coast are many, thus in recent years logs as well as cut lumber lost from these operations drifts into the sea then is distributed on the beach by the tides. In the 1970's, the driftwood pileup at Battle Rock is substantial and fanciers of it have the Northwest's huge timber industry to thank. One might conclude that the lack of driftwood at Battle Rock in early photos (p.21) is because there were so few lumber mills in the early days. *See;* Webber, Bert and Margie, "Identifying Driftwood," in *Beachcombing and Camping Along the Northwest Coast* (Ye Galleon Press) 1978.

in 1855 on Rogue River in defending her house and home containing the dead body of her husband and her living child, when for more than ten hours she, all alone, stood off at least one hundred of the bravest Indians that ever lifted a white man's scalp, killing, according to the Indians' own statement, fifteen. To this little woman we must all give the praise of making the grandest fight, against fearful odds, that was ever made on the continent of America.

It was the first time that the Indians of Port Orford had ever been whipped, usually killing more of the white men than they themselves had had killed. Here they had lost 25 warriors and not killed or captured a single white man. It was the old cannon that did the work. It was an entirely new thing to them as they really

Sea Captain Tichenor's grave overlooks the Pacific Ocean from atop a hill west of Port Orford city center.

thought that we were using thunder and lightning against them. The noise and the fearful execution done by the gun demoralized them. They were not only scared but they were terrified and the killing of their two big chiefs taught them that we were dangerous. I have often thought that our escape was due as much to their fear of us as to our good luck. I can look back over the long stretch of years and feel a generous pride that none of my party were killed.

I know not if any of my old comrades are living now. I was the youngest one in the party and I have passed my three score and ten. If any of them are living, "God's blessing on them;" if they have crossed the great Divide, then "Farewell."

Nearly all of the old pioneers of Oregon are gone. No braver, bigger-hearted, or truer set of pioneers ever blazed the way for the march of civilization than they who,

> "Belonged to the legion that never were listed,
> They carried no banner nor crest;
> But, split in a thousand detachments,
> Were breaking the ground for the rest."

My task is done, and I claim no other merit for these recollections than that of truth.

J.M. KIRKPATRICK.

Oregon Territorial Handstamps used in Post Offices about the time of the founding of Port Orford.

Umpqua City: Opened Sept. 26, 1851. Amos E. Rogers, Postmaster. (Closed March 19, 1869)
Portland: Opened Nov. 8, 1849. Thomas Smith, Postmaster
Port Orford: Opened March 27, 1855. Reginald H. Smith, Postmaster
—from Payne List of *Oregon Post Offices and First Postmasters* (n.d.)

Port Orford Post Office in 1977.

DISCOVERY OF RICH GOLD FIELDS.

After much delay Captain Tichenor returned to Port Orford and found with dismay that there had been a battle with the Indians, and that the men he had left in charge were either killed or had escaped.

The Indians were finally subdued, and it was discovered that there was vast stretches of black sand on the beach, reaching from Coos Bay southward to Crescent City. These sands were permeated with fine particles of gold, and many fortunes were made with the "TOM" process; but the miners began to follow up the stream, believing that the gold found on the beach came from a mineral belt that existed in the mountains. Johnsons Creek, a stream heading at Salmon Mountain, proved to be very rich, and coarse gold soon found its way into the miners' sack. The streamer being only a few miles in length it was soon worked out, as the rush to that new Eldorado was great. After taking out many thousand dollars, the prospectors broke camp and started for other fields of promise. Had these adventurers gone three miles to the head of one of the branches of the stream and examined the foothills for quartz, they would have found mines that afterwards became noted for their vast wealth. In after years, while working on the side of Salmon Mountain in a placer mine, Mr. Dunbar uncovered ore or quartz that yielded wonderful results. One piece that weighed two hundred pounds yielded $2,700 and other analysis showed a value as high at $600 per ton. The placer mine thus worked yielded good results in coarse gold and amalgum, and besides ore of different grades were uncovered, but a forest fire sweeping over the mountain destroyed their three miles of flume and all other improvements that were of a nature susceptible to destruction.

The owners of this valuable property concluded to transfer it to more energetic hands, hence a company was formed, capitalizing at only $50,000, 25,000 shares being placed on the market to enable the company to adopt improved methods so that the gold might be secured rapidly and at the least expense.

DESCRIPTION OF THE MINE.

The mine is known as Salmon Mountain Placer Mine and owned by the Salmon Mountain Coarse Gold Mining Company, their principal place of busienss being at Myrtle Point, Oregon, near Coos Bay. The company has 300 acres. It lays on the north slope of Salmon Mountain, situated near the county line dividing Coos and Curry counties in southwest Oregon. The mine is 30 miles from Myrtle Point, a thriving town situated at the head of navigation on the Coquille River, a stream that joins the Pacific Ocean 25 miles north of Port Orford. There is a line of steamers running between Coos Bay and San Francisco, and Myrtle Point is connected by railroad with Coos Bay, and a wagon road connects Myrtle Point with the mine.

★　　★　　★　　★　　★

REPORT OF THE U.S. GEOLOGICAL SURVEYOR AND MINERALOGIST, PORT ORFORD, OREGON, FOLIO NO. 89, PUBLISHED BY THE DEPARTMENT OF THE INTERIOR.

"The Salmon Mountain Mine on the north slope of Salmon Mountain, at an elevation of 2,100 feet, is hydraulic, using water with nearly 200 feet head, brought across the divide from the upper part of Johnsons Creek. The cut is about 50 feet deep, the same in width, and 500 feet long, with a range of 200 feet in hight. It is in rather fragmental material of igneous origin, except at the lower end, where Eocene shales and sandstone occur. Although closed at the present time, it has been worked during the rainy seaosn at intervals for a number of years. When running under a good head the mine paid $75 to $100 a day and the gold is said to be rather uniformly distributed through the whole mass."

These facts have been set forth so that those who wish to make an investment in a very promising proposition can do so. It is confidently believed that this is as good and safe a field for such an enterprise as can be found and those contemplating such an investment should apply in person or by letter addressed to the Secretary of the company, Mr. Orvil Dodge, Myrtle Point, Oregon, and proper blanks will be furnished.

All of the stock offered is Treasury stock, and only so much will be sold as will be sufficient to equip the mine.

If you have a hundred or a thousand to invest you are face to face with an opportunity for rich returns that is little likely to occur again in your lifetime. If you want to act on this proposition, prompt, immediate subscription is the only sure way to secure the stock.

Following is an extract from a letter written by Hon. Binges Herman, ex-Commissioner of the General Land Office, and now a Member of Congress:

"I have known the Salmon Mountain Mine forty years at least, and have known of its great mineral wealth. I have known of large quantities of coarse gold having been extracted. * * * I know all of the people who constitute the ownership of this valuable property and know them to be men of integrity and responsibility in the community in which they reside. * * * I have confidence in the extent and richness of the Salmon Mountain Mine."

51

FIRST QUARTERLY REPORT TO THE STOCK-HOLDERS OF THE SALMON MOUNTAIN COARSE GOLD MINING CO.

★

Principle place of business, Myrtle Point, Oreg.

(Incorporated under the laws of the State of Oregon.)

December 31, 1903.

The mine originally consisted of 8 placer claims, to which 4 more have been added. The company has recently secured 4 quartz claims, which have been developed while working the placer mine, they being on the same ground.

The assay of the quartz lodes thus found is officially reported by Professor Monroe, of the Columbian University, of Washington, D.C., as able to produce the following results:

$$
\begin{aligned}
&\text{Ore No. 1} \ldots\ldots\ldots\ldots\ldots \$268.88 \text{ per ton} \\
&\text{Ore No. 2} \ldots\ldots\ldots\ldots\ldots\ 243.50 \text{ per ton} \\
&\text{Ore No. 3} \ldots\ldots\ldots\ldots\ldots\ 600.80 \text{ per ton} \\
&\text{Ore No. 4} \ldots\ldots\ldots\ldots\ldots\ \ \ 8.03 \text{ per ton}
\end{aligned}
$$

The samples thus analyzed were selected by persons not interested, and an affidavit of two men set forth the fact that they were fair and true samples of the mine.

The improvements on the mine now consist of 1 sawmill (water power), 1 giant, a blacksmith shop (well equipped), boarding house, large warehouse, 1 steam boiler and engine, eraster, 3 miles of flume, about 400 yards of sluice-boxes, picks, shovels, and other tools to work 10 men. There is about 1,500 feet of tunneling, that proves the value and extent of the mine to be excellent and a good investment.

During the last quarter the company have caused to be expended on the mine, preparing for large improvements, the sum of $1,000, so they will be ready to put in the necessary machinery to equip the mine and have it in good working order by the 1st of next July, when a surprising dividend may be looked for, within the year.

As soon as shares are sold and a few thousand dollars are realized, a stamp mill will be placed on the premises and run night and day, in charge of an expert.

Several thousand more shares are being taken by persons in Myrtle Point and vicinity, who personally know the value of the property.

As soon as operations are under way you will receive another report, which will be made quarterly thereafter.

Orvil Orvando Dodge (1839—1914), compiler of *Pioneer History of Coos and Curry Counties* (1898), *The Heroes of Battle Rock* (1904) and Secretary of Salmon Mountain Coarse Gold Mining Company, was a newspaper editor and historian who was educated in New York and Indiana. He arrived in Oregon in 1861 by way of California and served in the First Oregon Cavalry. After being wounded, he was discharged to become at the age of 24, a traveling photographer. He gave up the camera in 1866 to be a merchant at Empire City but in 1870 he moved to the Coquille Valley where he served as U.S. Commissioner at Myrtle Point (1889-1903). He published two newspapers there. Dodge was married twice. He had two children by his first wife and six by his second.

—Extracted from Corning, H.W.,*Dictionary of Oregon History*.

OFFICERS AND MEMBERS SALMON MOUNTAIN COARSE GOLD MINING COMPANY.

Name	Address
B. Fenton, *President,*	Myrtle Point, Oreg.
John J. Curren, *First Vice-President*	Myrtle Point, Oreg.
C.C. Carter, *Second Vice-President*	Myrtle Point, Oreg.
Orvil Dodge, *Secretary*	Myrtle Point, Oreg.
M. R. Lee, *Assistant Secretary,*	Myrtle Point, Oreg.
R. W. Lundy, *Treasurer,*	Myrtle Point, Oreg.
T. M. Hermann, *Corresponding Sec'y,*	Myrtle Point, Oreg.
Norman Dodge, *Engineer,*	Myrtle Point, Oreg.
Stephen Gallier, *Sheriff of Coos Co.,*	Coquille City, Oreg.
E. Galliger, *Deputy Sheriff of Coos Co.,*	Coquille City, Oreg.

Coast Guardsmen with war dogs were stationed at Port Orford during World War II where they walked the beaches rain or shine, day and night on the lookout for unauthorized persons. (Photo p. 56) The threat of invasion along many of the Pacific Northwest's "vulnerable" beaches was great, according to the military leaders, but no enemy came. (Left) Beach hut of driftwood served as rest station for weary Guardsmen who carried rifles as well as special radios adapted from the U.S. Forest Service. (Right) War dogs were trained to attack anyone they could reach except for their own handler.

Port Orford did not escape excitement during World War II. On October 5, 1942, Richfield Oil Company tanker *Larry Doheny* was sunk by Japanese submarine *I-25* off Cape Sebastion about thirty miles south of Port Orford. Rescue vessels put survivors ashore at Port Orford the following evening.

On November 7, the Coast Guard established a Beach Patrol unit and barracks at Port Orford then immediately, with war dogs, combed the beaches and scaled cliffs on a day and night schedule guarding against invasion. The unit was disbanded on March 29, 1944.

Not revealed to the people of Port Orford or to the U.S. military until 1975, is the incident where submarine *I-25* on September 9, 1942, crept along the ocean floor and took refuge in Port Orford harbor — on the bottom! The submarine, which carried an aircraft, had completed the first enemy bombing of the U.S. mainland in history had itself been attacked by an A-29 patrol bomber as the sub was making a routine dive after recovering its own aircraft. (*I-25* had been damaged by the A-29 but the American pilot did not know he'd hit it until 1974.) The Japanese plane had dropped bombs on Siskiyou National Forest, east of Brookings, and started a forest fire. American surface ships depth charged *I-25* (all missed) as Commander Meiji Tagami quietly moved his leaking submarine along the bottom "one meter at a time to the safety of Port Orford." The next day Tagami put to sea and engaged in additional adventures before his return to Japan. *See:* Webber, Bert, *Retaliation: Japanese Attacks and Allied Countermeasures Along the Pacific Coast in World War II* (Oregon State University Press, Corvallis). The quote from Mr. Tagami to Webber during the reception in Tokyo July 31, 1975, for Bert and Margie Webber. About thirty former submarine men, including the pilot attended.

REPORT of THE SUPERINTENDENT of the COAST SURVEY during 1858

Port Orford:

This is by far the best summer roadstead on the coast between Los Reyes and the Strait of Juan de Fuca. From the extremity of the SW. point eastward to the main shore the distance is two miles, and from this line to the greatest bend of the shore northward the distance is one mile. The soundings within this space range from 16 fathoms close to Tichenor's Rock, forming the SW. point of the bay, to 3 fathoms within one-quarter of a mile of the beach on the northeast side; with 5 fathoms at the base of the rocky points on the northwest side towards Tichenor's Rock, one mile off the shores of the bay, the average depth is about 14 fathoms, regularly decreasing inshore.

The point forming the western part of the bay presents a very rugged, precipitous outline, and attains an elevation of 350 feet. Its surface is covered with excellent soil and with a sparse growth of fir. From this point the shore becomes depressed to about 60 feet at the northern or middle part of the shore of the bay where the town is located. The hills behind are covered with a thick growth of fir and cedar.

The anchorage is usually made with the eastern end of the town bearing north, being just open to the east of a high rock on the beach, in 6 fathoms water, hard bottom; having a sharp, high point bearing NW. by W. one-quarter of a mile distant, the beach in front of the town distant a quarter of a mile; and three rocks just in the three-fathom line E. by N., distant half a mile. Steamers anchor a little to the eastward of this position, and closer to the town, in 4 fathoms. Coasters from the south in summer beat up close inshore, stretching inside of the outlying islets to avoid the heavy swell outside. Coming from the northward they keep just outside of a high rock one-third of a mile off the western head, and round Tichenor's Rock within a half a mile. In winter anchor far enough out to be ready to put to sea when a southeaster comes up. During a protracted gale in December, 1851, a terrible sea rolled in that no vessel could have ridden out. The old Steamer *Sea Gull* was driven northward, and lost two weeks in regaining her position, and the mail steamer *Columbia* hardly held her own for many hours off the Orford reef.

The usual landing is between the rock called Battle Rock, north of the anchorage, and the point of rock close on its west side. A road is cut from here up to the town, which consists of but a few houses. Sometimes a landing is made on the rocky beach a quarter of a mile westward of Battle Rock, in the bight where a sloping grassy bluff comes to the water; but this landing is over a rocky bottom. A road is cut up the slope to the site of the military post of Port Orford, which is now abandoned.

The primary astronomical station of the Coast Survey, established here in 1851, is on the top of the ridge just west of the town, at a height of 262 feet above the sea, and within a few yards of the western edge of the bluff. Its geographical position is:

Latitude..........................42°44'21.7" north.
Longitude.................................124°28'47" west.

Magnetic variation 18° 29' east, in November, 1851, with a yearly increase of about 1'.4. From this station Tichenor's Rock bears S. by W., three quarters of a mile distant.

The secondary astronomical station (1853) is in front of the town, north of Battle Rock, and within 50 yards of the edge of the bluff. Its geographical position is:

Latitude......................42°44'28.2" north.
Longitude.....................124°28'13" west.

The Pacific Ocean. Camera faces north from edge of cliff northwest of Old Coast Guard Station.

PHOTO CREDITS

Many of the pictures appearing in this book, although borrowed from and credited to others, were made in the compiler's photolab in Medford, Oregon, from micro-copyfilm to preserve the originals. Photos not credited were taken by the compiler.

v(left) from Gaston
  (right) Evelyne Michael
viii (Left) E. Michael
  (right) Ruby Van Deventer
xiii (top) Margie Shoemaker
  (bottom left and right) City of Port Orford
xiv-xv City of Port Orford
xvi (right) Lauren T. Webber
17 from Gaston
18-19 from Dodge (1898)
20 *Harper's Weekly*
21 Curry County Historical Society (C.C.H.S.)

22 From Gaston
23 *Harper's Weekly*
24-25 C.C.H.S.
26 Louis L. Knapp
27-30 C.C.H.S.
34 C.C.H.S.
41 (top) City of Port Orford
43 Minnie King Jolly
46 C.C.H.S. (Neva Chenoweth Boyd)
53 from Gaston
54 Glen Barkhurst, Jr.
Back Cover: Dale B. Webber

INDEX

Page numbers in *italic* are illustrations.